Going to School

A TODDLER PREP™ BOOK

Ready SetPrep

About Toddler Prep™ Books

The best way to prepare a child for any new experience is to help them understand what to expect beforehand, according to experts. And while cute illustrations and fictional dialogue might be entertaining, little ones need a more realistic representation to fully understand and prepare for new experiences.

With Toddler Prep™ Books, a series by ReadySetPrep™, you can help your child make a clear connection between expectation and reality for all of life's exciting new firsts. Born from firsthand experience and based on research from leading developmental psychologists, the series was created by Amy and Aaron Pittman – parents of two who know (all too well) the value of preparation for toddlers.

You're going to school! There will be so many fun things to see and do. Let's talk about what happens when you go to school.

School is where you go to learn fun things and make new friends.

Before you go to school, you have to get ready. In the morning, you wake up and get dressed.

Then, we brush your teeth and fix your hair.

We gather your things. You can bring your blanket, teddy bear, or any other special cuddly object for nap time.

When you're ready to go, we drive to school and go inside.

We walk into your classroom and say hello to your teacher. They will be so happy to see you! Do you know your teacher's name?

Your teacher keeps you safe and helps you have fun. It's important to listen to your teacher just like you listen to me.

After we say hi to your teacher, we put your things away in your cubby.

SCHOOL

Then it's time for me to leave. What special way should we say goodbye? We can hug, kiss, or give a high five.

It's ok if you feel a little sad or nervous when I leave. You're going to have so much fun and I *always* come back at the end of the day to pick you up.

SCHOOL

The best part about school is you make lots of new friends. You play games and do fun activities all day!

You play with new toys, paint pictures, and sing funny songs.

And you go outside to play on a playground every day!

You learn so many new things
at school too—like numbers,
letters, and shapes.

It's important to follow the rules so everyone stays safe. Listen to your teacher, be kind and gentle to the other kids, and clean up your toys.

At school, there is a potty you can use.
If you need help, just ask your teacher.

During lunch and snack time, you eat at little tables with chairs that are just your size.

In the afternoon, you take a break from playing and take a nap. You have a soft mat to lie on so you're nice and comfy.

During nap time, it's important to lie still and stay quiet so your body is rested and ready for more fun in the afternoon.

Sometimes you have story time. You sit on the floor and listen to your teacher read a book.

SCHOOL

Soon it is time for me to pick you up! On the way home, you tell me all about the fun things you did.

You did it! Now you know how to go to school.

Made in United States
Cleveland, OH
25 September 2024

10080695R20017